reality.

by Eleni Theocharopoulos

an *lni* book by  turtle concept

I really wonder, I do.

Will the day come I'll see through

Through the light of your eyes, through your soul

Will I let go my love and free my heart

Will it meet yours? Will they become one?

Sometimes my thoughts wander

To a playground so far away in time

I try to remember, I barely can

And here I am

There is no reason to hope

Nothing to expect

The emptiness of the dark

Only fills my heart with an unconditional love

A smooth bliss and a sweet warmth

Like lava

Slowly descending the mountain,

Burning every ambition, every foreign creation

It is not their world my love

Yet they are so present.

These monsters with their boots trespassing the rivers

Never getting wet,

They fill with mud every spring they find

Make roofs to protect you from the rain, from the sun

Their life takes its roots in yours

And they feed from your crops

Tiny soldiers of the dark

They too seek the shine

To find glory in possession

To find rest in control

Tiny soldiers will battle for instant comfort

Short seeing is indeed an awful disease

They will never cross the border,

They will not take the moment to look into your eyes

To see you

To feel you

To bring you comfort

Tiny soldiers will find comfort

A round ring, a union of the people

And then there is you and I my love,

The round ring

Tiny soldiers show a path

A way to their light

Ignorance guides you towards the flame,

Hunger for knowledge,

Hunger for deliverance

So much potential, and so little help

All this time I travel fiercely

Courageously, passionately, and respectfully

Listening to others, risking for others

No ego, only faith in finding you

Your eyes, your lips, your breath

And tiny soldiers are still around

They show the path

They show the light

I follow, I lead, I see the flame

And I cannot see you

I pass by.

It is not my light

It has become yet another shadow

I look around and see satisfaction, fulfillment

Little soldiers are growing; their shine is expanding,

A shadow has been added

I feel the lava descend

Warm and slow

It is the ultimate shadow

Destroying all shadows of the heart

There is no tomorrow for you and me

There is only now

No past, no future

No projections

No expectations

No need for hope

Love is present

I look into your eyes and I take a step

I allow myself to open my eyes in this garden

I have so naturally entered

I look, I contemplate

I discover your colors

I discover your flowers, trees, and fruits

I can see the wild beasts

And the tender ones as well

I let myself flow

I breathe in; not wanting to breathe out

Keeping your garden forever in me

In my heart

I wonder if you see me

Standing

Contemplating

Now that my heart is no more

Time can stop life my love

And life can stop time

Take a moment to breathe

To be seen

To be contemplated

Let me fill your heart with my love,

Let me add my colors to yours

Let me bring music with me

Let me touch you

And lets...!

My light has awakened your beasts

And the shadows do rest no more

Please let them growl, let them bark

Let them rise and fall

They will get used to the change

Our world is new

Our world is rebellious

Transparent to soldiers;

It does not belong to time

Only to the eternity of the moment

Standing on the rock

The ocean around me is blue

Sometimes green, sometimes white

I am free

Standing on the rock

The breeze fills my heart with faith

Peace is all around me, peace is within

Peace is between you and I

A small child is born

He is the rebel of our humanity

The rebel against the soldiers

The rebel stands strong
The rebel never hides

In a world of dictators
The rebel is silently present
Little soldiers campaign against him
And make him invisible to all
But you and I have now the freedom to see him

If only we dared to open our eyes

Now and then the rebel manifests
Winning small battles
Bringing small lights into darker spaces
Showing a different path

The rebel has roots in you my love

Your soul, your heart

The intensity of their power unlocks all gates

Take a moment to meet him

The purity of his existence

The majesty of his presence

Make it so difficult to look him in the eyes

To accept him, to believe such great beauty is possible

He is present when the sun rises

Present when the flower blossoms

Present when you look at me

The rebel is always present

Like a child who dances
And smiles, and twirls
And laughs

Like the dolphin who kept company to the small boat
We used to take to escape
Swimming around us
Greeting our love with such purity
It only made it stronger

The rebel looks over you and I

When our soul is in need

And our heart is questioning every beat

When certain is not an option any more

And something deep inside

Offers the confidence it will all be all right

The rebel comes to you

As if every breath of your body is calling his name

And he will give more

More than the little soldiers have promised

Do you remember

When the little soldiers made you enter

Even darker areas

To reach the flame so vividly promised?

Quite controversial my love

Taking you deeper in the darkness of the night

With the mere lure of a twilight

The rebel on the other hand my love

Will show you the morning sun

He takes you straight to happiness

He gives relief

The rebel listens to you

To your heart

To you soul

It does come as a surprise at first

For sure

When you open the door

And greet the possibility

The infinity of serendipity

The stretch of the heart

Have you ever felt this way my love?

Walking for days so lightly

Floating just a hair above the ground

The dizziness of the wonder

Makes your mind still

Silence has a new kingdom

Your mind is finally infertile of any thought

Ceasing every interaction

While it unites with the environment

Your heart is sparkling

Feeling all is possible

Daring to wish under the shooting stars

Daring for a slight moment to believe

You are riding one of them

You are not alone my love

The rebel is there

Walking next to you

Holding your hand

When in fact

You are holding his

Standing by your side

Listening to your heart

The rebel has always been there

Waiting for you to tune in

Nothing brings me more peace

Than the moment I surrender

And let him take care of me

All this time I had the choice my love

The freedom to see the world

The freedom to listen

The freedom to believe

I could have looked at the colors

And the beauty of the fish

And the tranquility the river had to offer

I could have felt the thin air that kept me awake

Instead I was giving all my attention

All my energy to the trunk that was blocking the pace

Making the water rough and dusty at parts

It is possible not to enter the corridor

Not to ask for the exit

Not to accept their path

It is possible to look at life

Like a child in the playground

The truth has never been one

The truth is built by rebels and by soldiers

The choice my love is your gift

You can either enter the land holding the rebel's hand

Or keep company with the beasts

I have been sitting with the beasts for too long

I now can stand and look at the waters

Standing on the rock, I hold his hand

The rock looks like the smallest pebble at first

Growing every day like the most exotic shell

The more you stand strong,

The more you hold his hand

The more the rock expands, creating a new land

The land is wild

The land is fertile

Slightly visible through the morning mist

You can barely see it

Like a dream, like a vision

It appears and disappears

Hold on to the rebel's hand

Even if the sight is blurry

Leaving the little soldiers to invade the moment

Will only take you away

The rebel will guide you to the land

Keep walking my love

Little soldiers have no business here

They are trained to interfere

To show you the shine of darkness

They will cast you out to punish you

They will feed your beasts

And pain will rise

Hold the rebel's hand my love
Not many can follow their path
Not many can accept their defeat
And support you in your journey
Their pain is too strong to bear
They have to let go of your hand

It is your path to walk today

The shores of the land will always welcome you

You can set foot anytime

And stay as long as you like

The beat of your heart changes

It is neither faster nor slower

Neither stronger nor weaker

It is just different

Synchronization is key

Feel the land

Smell its perfume

Touch its soil

Hear its song

Tune into its energy

Infuse into its core

Be part of the land my love

Let your gravity take a new dimension

Let the Southern Cross hold your feet

And the North Star flirt with your head

Your body, your heart, your mind and soul

Create an invisible bridge

Between the green and the sapphire

You naturally stand tall my love

Very well grounded

Your heart can finally stretch

Reaching places you have never been before

Offering your love, compassion, adoration, help

Offering your values to others with no holding back

The rebel is still there

The land is fertile

Keep walking my love

It is all clear around,

No clouds, no shadows

Only the colors of the rainbow

Perfectly balanced

Perfectly communicating with each other

You shine my love

I can see the light

You are so beautiful

So peaceful

You look at me with your soul

You understand

You see the path I have travelled

The shadows that have invaded me

You accept

The little soldiers do not bother you anymore

Now and then they come to the shores

Looking for the beasts

Waking them up

And you let them growl, you let them bark

Taking a small step aside to let them pass by

You look at them and let them be

The little soldiers have risen and they have fallen

The rebel has taught you well

To Zoe & to Lilly
who both have helped in their own,
very different and unique way.

And a very special thank you to Torie
who has helped and supported me
in making this book happen.

an lni book by turtle concept
ISBN 978-2-8399-1142-9
November 2012